BRICKYARD SUMMER

A Richard Jackson Book

BRICKYARD SUMMER

Poems by **Paul B. Janeczko**

Illustrated by Ken Rush

49881

Orchard Books · New York

A division of Franklin Watts, Inc.

Orchard Books
A division of Franklin Watts, Inc.
387 Park Avenue South
New York, NY 10016

Manufactured in the United States of America
Book design by Tere LoPrete

10   9   8   7   6   5   4   3   2   1

The text of this book is set in 11 pt. Linotype Walbaum.
The illustrations are black-and-white oil paintings reproduced in halftone.

Library of Congress Cataloging-in-Publication Data
Janeczko, Paul B.
    Brickyard summer.

    "A Richard Jackson book"—
    Summary: In a series of poems, the speaker and his best friend meander through the summer after eighth grade, encountering for the first time in the local people of their economically depressed neighborhood enormous courage and vitality.
    1. Children's poetry, American. [1. American poetry.   2. City and town life—Poetry]   I. Rush, Ken, ill.   II. Title.
PS3560.A465B75   1989   811'.54   89-42542
ISBN 0-531-05846-8
ISBN 0-531-08446-9 (lib. bdg.)

For Nadine

queen of the slipstream
my tupelo honey
I'm in heaven when you smile

with love

Contents

V

VI

BRICKYARD SUMMER

Brickyard

Four stories,
two blocks long,
the mill sat
across Cedar from the Brickyard,
named for the way
our white clapboard triple deckers
caught the rose wash
from the mill
in early morning light.

From the corner room on the top floor
I watched
workers with black lunch pails,
delivery trucks,
a slow train carrying cloth

and the sun shining
on the coins of summer days.

Bonfire

That summer
school ended
with a half-day Tuesday.
But before baseball
    fishing
        reading comics
           tenting out
we carried notebooks, tests, and compositions
to a cleared spot
at the edge of the ball field
and began the tearing and crumpling of pages:
the quiz we took the morning
Mrs. Hamilton backed her black Buick
over her trash cans;
the report on flax I delivered
the day of the hurricane,
when a wedge of the ceiling collapsed
on the Blessed Virgin
and we prayed;
the composition Raymond wrote
the day he wore his mother's blonde wig to school;
teeth-marked yellow pencils—
mostly no. 2s with flat erasers;
and penmanship workbooks
filled with the proper swirls and curls.
Even holy cards
of robed smileless saints
and lists of spelling demons
were ready to burn.

One wooden match
struck on my belt buckle
was enough
to start the flames
that let
eighth grade dance
away.

Firsts

In the South Street Pool Hall,
got as far as the chest
of bottles of Coke and Nehi
bobbing with ice
before Earl,
the one-eared manager growled,
"That's as far as you go
'less you're small
for your age."

Spotted a flock of bras
hanging from the line
behind the convent;
passed on Raymond's dare
to snag one.

Lost a bet
with Wanda Sterling
that she couldn't hold fifty pennies
in her mouth
for a minute.

Watched as they carried
Mrs. Carter covered
from her house;
heard people say,
"Things got to be too much."

Felt a buzz of electricity
when Raymond's Ouija board
spelled out
I would meet a girl named Jane
the first week of high school.

Raymond

Hair the color of pencil shavings,
eyes as dark as a night river,
best friend
since fifth grade
when he seemed to stop
growing.

Large enough
to blacken Danny Webb's eye
when he said,
"Hiya, pipsqueak,"
the first day of eighth grade,

small enough
to get into the movies as a kid.

At the Top Hat Café,
gave me one play
on his juke box quarters.

For three nights,
trusted me
with the false teeth
(uppers only)
he found
on a park bench.

In The Tattoo Emporium,
let me help him
pick out the
eagle-holding-thunderbolt
he'd claim for his chest
the day he turned eighteen.

Glass-Eye Harry Coote

Glass-Eye Harry Coote lost it
in a mill accident.

From his park bench
where he could see time pass
on the city hall tower clock,
he claimed
for twenty-five cents
he would look
into your soul
and see your strength.

I tried it once
with Raymond watching.
Laid a quarter in his hand.
Glass-Eye looked into my soul
while his good eye
stared at the quarter until he told me,
"Your strength is friendship."

Silent until we passed from the park,
Raymond muttered,
"Should be against the law
to take money
for telling something
as plain as bark on a tree."
I said nothing,
gladly still hearing
the words both had spoken.

Bad

Passing high-school kids
hanging out in front of Manny's,
leaning against
Impalas,
parking meters,
each other,
I remembered the nuns' warnings
of a world of black and white
as frequent as weather reports
on the radio,
as much a part of the classroom
as the squeak of their shoes,
the click of their beads.
Finally, in May, Sister Mary Ellen,
who smelled like our attic,
hoisted a storm warning—

"It will be easier to be bad
in high school,"
she told us
and then explained how:
Necking
    petting
       dancing
          drinking
             dirty books
                impure thoughts
                   missing Mass
                      wasting time
                        cigarettes
                          condemned movies

and
the Seven Deadly Sins—
especially lust.
Especially lust.

I moved on quickly,
anxious for the storm.

Mystery

One Friday night
Mom pulled out
Learning to Dance Is Fun
with diagrams of feet
and a long-play record,
while Dad watched,
like a patient
awaiting
the dentist's whining drill.

Mom counted softly
onetwo
onetwothree
through
    fox trot
        samba
            cha-cha-cha
as Dad danced—
feet on the wrong legs.

Yet,
the next afternoon
before the ball left the bat
Dad danced deep
into the hole at short,
lunged,
backhanded
in the middle of a bad hop—
the ball
at the edge of the webbing—
then
twirling,
falling away:
a perfect peg
to first.

Ruth

At the Top Hat Café
Raymond and I perched on counter stools
like gulls on a pier
and watched Ruth split eggs
one-handed on the edge of the grill,
quietly,
with barely a click,
with the suddenness of a magician
flicking flashy silks
from your pocket
or shiny coins
from your ear.
We hated to take our eyes off
her hands.

For a finale,
Ruth tossed the shells
into the dented galvanized bucket
without looking.
Nothing flamboyant,
just a quick flip
behind her back.

It was enough
to make me laugh
at talk of dancers and swans.

Gus

Gus was slow.
Too slow
for Mrs. Scott
who stopped most afternoons
for coffee and Danish
on the way home from the bank.
"Can't you hurry?"
she asked, as Gus poured coffee
into a white Styrofoam cup
with Sweet Tooth Bakery
swirled on it.

We all,
except Mrs. Scott,
who was mining for coins
in her purse,
saw the bluebottle,
fat and lazy,
circle Gus,
and we all,
except Mrs. Scott,
knew where it was going
to end up.
Which it did
a blink before she looked
up and said, "Well?"
to Gus holding the lid.
Gus looked at us,
at her,
when she ordered,
"Put the lid on!"
which he did after
looking at us again,
his eyes saying,
You heard her.

We watched her hurry
to her Lincoln
that leaped away from the curb
as another bluebottle buzzed
in the front window
and Gus said,
"Sometimes you have to know
when the customer is always right."

Dancers

Miss Beemis never married.
"I can't *begin* to count the men
who asked me,"
she in high heels told us one Saturday
while we carried her trash.
"Too busy teaching ballroom dancing
in nineteen states,"
she said,
paying us
with peanut-butter cookies
in her yellow kitchen.
"Not that I'm lonely," she laughed
as she walked to her hi-fi
and set a record playing.
"Why, I have a *trunk* of memories."

"Let me show you my stuff," she said.
Not sure what she meant, we nodded,
and she slipped into a dress
the color of creamed corn
that rustled like a grass fire.
"This is the dress that drove men wild,
absolutely wild."
Which I couldn't believe
until she bent over the cookies,
snatched my hand,
let me peer into her
delicious darkness.

"Feel the music," she crooned
and swept me
as graceful as a coat rack
away.

Sundays

For lunch
Dad wore a white shirt
with cuffs stiff
as the ace of spades,
knit pants,
and loafers.

After lunch
we walked to the park
as he rubbed the baseball
with hands as tough and smooth
as the underside of a tortoise.

At the backstop,
as slowly as bread rising,
he rolled up his sleeves
before hitting fly balls
that seemed to skip off the sun
before landing
still warm
in my mitt.

The Poet

Before he moved in with Miss Perry,
the librarian—
    whose perfume we knew *had* to come from Paris,
        whose smile dazzled and made us look away,
           whose clothes let us imagine secrets—
he stayed mostly by the benches
in front of the library
reciting poems
across from the Lucky Seven Bar & Grille
where Raymond said he got his inspiration.

Until Miss Perry
complained to the police
that the man, as Raymond's mom had heard it,
was pestering her patrons.

With Yankee cap in hand
he faced Miss Perry at the circulation desk:

"Let me untie the stars,
  string them like so many dreams
  on a silver chain of raindrops
  and dance my necklace round your fair, thin neck.
  (deep breath)
  Let me make for you a cape
  to wrap you in my madman dreams
  embroidered with the silk thread of memories,
  bordered by the lace of our love."

She blushed,
sat,
stammered,
"All right all right,
  but you must do it quietly."

And that easily we lost her.

21

Stories

Old Lester Darby,
thin as wire,
sat at a card table,
retirement pocket watch ticking
next to a half-completed
jigsaw puzzle of Mount Rushmore,
and told hours of stories about baseball
and the days he played
with the St. Louis Browns
back, as he said, when
players weren't a bunch of sissies,

about fanning Ruth and Gehrig in '28,
about long smoky train rides in sleeper cars,
about ladies who loved pitchers.

Until Raymond looked him up
in the *Baseball Encyclopedia*
in the library
and found nothing.

When we went to ask him
why he did it,
Lester Darby,
waiting with lemonade on the porch
as the sun slid home,
said, "Did I ever tell you about the time
I got in a fist fight with Ty Cobb
in a hotel in Detroit?"
And we decided the stories
were better than the truth.

Lecture

We couldn't escape
Raymond's Aunt Clare,
an art teacher from Boston,
who lectured us at lunch
on still-life paintings
and demonstrated
the proper placement of a napkin,
the correct grip on a knife when cutting,
the right way to chew food,
until Raymond
let slip a fart,
silent
yet suddenly apparent
as a marching band.

Aunt Clare sniffed,
stood,
said she thought she'd left the iron on,
and left us
to duel with our forks
until our napkins skidded to the floor,
milk dribbled from our mouths,
and the dishes rattled
with our silent laughter.

Roscoe

Mrs. Carlucci's cat,
a calico whose belly kissed the ground,
stayed away
even though she stuck her head out the window,
thick glasses perched on the end of her nose,
and called, "Roscoe!"
every day
while pinching off dead geranium blossoms.
Every day she asked,
"Did you boys see Roscoe?"
which we hadn't—
not since we chased him
down the alley behind the pawn shop,
until he died
with a choked screech under truck tires.
We hid him in the weeds,
one leg pointing home.

At the animal shelter we picked out a cat
that looked like Roscoe
and carried it to Mrs. Carlucci,
complete with our story
of how bullies had driven Roscoe away.

Mrs. Carlucci thanked us,
offered us a dollar each
for our lie.
"Take it,"
she said,
"for what you did."

She carried the calico inside
and we left,
lugging dollars
and the knowledge
of what we'd done.

The Word

The day Dad said
The Word
I couldn't have been more surprised
if I'd said it to him.
Cleaning the garage,
he gashed his hand
on a rusty hasp and said
it.
He looked at me.
I looked away
as if his pants had fallen down.

Knowing we knew The Word
left us wordless
until I shrugged loose two:
"It slipped."
"No excuse,"
he grumbled,
walked out
to treat his wound.

Reverend Mona

When the elders said she was too old,
Reverend Mona
surrendered her tabernacle
next to Fast Frankie's Pawn Shop
and dropped out of sight
long enough for people to wonder.
She returned,
a shaggy boat
leading a wake of dogs—
shepherd,
Husky,
mutts—
to preach on a bench
near a crescent of marigolds,
while her hounds sat,
a congregation in restless prayer.

I walked away
before our eyes could meet.

The Bridge

The railroad bridge
crossed the Royal River
but was not the way
we were supposed to cross
according to
nuns
        parents
            police
who declared the bridge unsafe.

But we did,
loud with victory
on the diamond near the mill,
bouncing a ball on the ties,
boasting of hot hits,
retelling the winning rally
in Red Barber's voice.

Two days later,
Marty Morgan—
chattery,
whip-armed shortstop—
fell through,
remained unfound
for two more.

The only words we said about it
were Raymond's
"We were lucky"
after we watched Marty
slide into the ambulance
wrapped in a rubber sheet.

Walker

Walker was what everybody called him
because he walked
and pushed
a shopping cart,
making frequent stops
to salvage
still-smokable cigarette butts;
to add
returnable bottles,
wheels,
and, now and then,
a kitchen sink.
Copper tubing was, he said, good as gold,
but you never had enough wire, rope, and two-by-fours.
We didn't know anybody
who'd ever been to his shack
although you could see it
out behind the tannery
past a break in the fence
wide enough for man and cart.

"Used to be a soldier,"
he told us as he lit a Lucky,
"till my back went out."
He spit
twice,
trying to get rid of tobacco
from the tip of his tongue.
"Tell you the truth,
I got sick of taking orders anyway.
Ain't no way to live."

His biggest find?
"That's easy:
  the rainy day
  I found the black magi,
  one hand missing,
  face chipped, showing white,
  out behind the public works garage,"
  then he added with a wink,
"and I gave him his first ride
  in a shopping cart."

Brothers

Raymond slowed
when he saw
Tommy Pape, Greg Dickey,
others old as Randy,
his baby brother,
who didn't wake up one morning.

He asked
when he saw
the face
in the oval silver frame on the TV,
"What if I forgot Randy?"
dead at four
three years ago.

When Raymond slept over
I awoke
to the deep music of moans,
crossed a patch of moonlit floor,
and pulled him
to the surface of his dream,
gasping tales of
a red toy tractor,
a kid with gray eyes.

History

The gargoyle
owner of Gold's Fix-It Shop
boasted,
"If it's broke,
I can fix it."
And he did
on the counter
where you could watch
while inhaling the perfume of 3-in-1
as you sat on twin fake leather chairs
with an ashtray between them.
Even the floor lamp
Mrs. Fecteau's drunk husband
had beaten for getting in his way.
Even the razor
(Such an imp!" he said
and shook his head)
Billy Peterson used
to shave stiff paint brushes
on his father's bench.

As he tinkered,
his sleeve crept up,
showing his history
tatooed on one wrist.

Some things remain forever broken.

The Monument

Henry Small stopped talking
the day after the cease-fire,
the day his son's plane
flamed from the sky.

He wouldn't talk
to me or Raymond
when we said hi to him
sitting on his porch
after work in the quarry,
beer in hand,
game crackling on his transistor;
or to the Assembly of God
women who offered him
tuna casseroles, cleanliness, and scriptures;
or to Mr. Randall
from the V.F.W.
who explained the new monument
and invited him to the dedication,
which Henry Small didn't attend.

The next dawn
an explosion cracked our sleep,
but no one knew what it was
until Glass-Eye Harry noticed
the momument gone,
the park littered with chunks of granite,
and called the police
who went to question Henry Small,
only to find his house empty
and Henry Small as gone as the monument.

Thieves

Inspired
by the heist in a
rainy Saturday afternoon movie
to pull our own job,
we agreed on the Buy-Rite Five & Dime,
decided on junk:
a pack of combs
and a card of thumbtacks,
since taking
something we wanted
would be too much like stealing.

Pretending we'd never met,
Raymond and I slipped into the store,
as comfortable as strolling into church,
him walking down the far aisle
past stationery, pet supplies, pots and pans,
me gliding by the snack bar
where two red-smocked workers
sipped coffee
from paper cups with pop-out handles.

Looking once
to make sure I was unnoticed,
to make sure Raymond wasn't watching me,
I dropped two packs of combs,
bent,
stuck one in my sock,
slapped the other back in the bin
before turning and walking
    slowly
        slowly
until I burst through the door,
a halfback through the line,
and raced down the street.

At the bench
in front of Fast Frankie's
we met,
giddy with triumph,
and swapped our booty,
poised for
    the sirens
        the bloodhounds
            the chase.

Spider

Spider always wore sunglasses
but we knew he wasn't blind,
not the way he moved
match to Marlboro,
raked a comb through his hair,
and smirked
when the girls from the high school
tried not to look at him
leaning against the hood
of his glossy black Impala.

He wore rumors
like the smell of cigarette smoke and Vitalis:
that he torpedoed the toilet at the Town Cinema,
that he swapped shots with police out west,
that Mr. Janelli fired him
when Spider stayed the afternoon with Mrs. Brewster
after delivering her groceries.

But it wasn't a rumor
the way he slouched against the bank
not letting kids pass—
"Do not pass Go. Do not collect $200—"
until they paid
a cigarette or change;
or that his hobbies included
making people walk around him,
pitching nickels behind Star Auto Parts,
working the pinball machine
until the ball blurred.

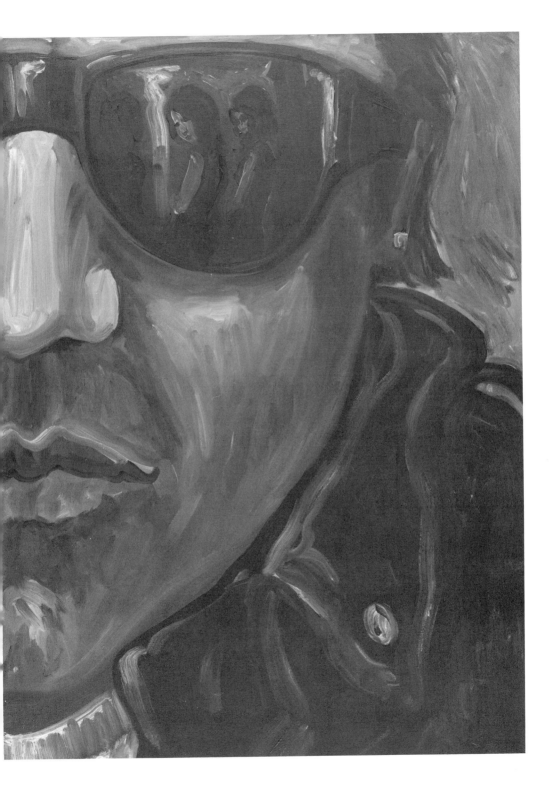

Hoods

In black leather jackets,
watching Spider work
the wire coat hanger
into Mrs. Koops's car,
they reminded me of crows
huddled around a road kill.
Startled,
they looked up,
then back
at Spider,
who nodded once,
setting them free
toward me.
I bounded away,
used a parking meter
to whip me around the corner
past Janelli's Market,
the darkened Pine Street Grille,
and the steamed windows
of Sudsy's Modern Laundromat.
I climbed—two at a time—
the granite steps
of the Free Public Library
and pushed back thick wooden doors
as the pursuing pack stopped—
sinners at the door of a church.

From the corner table of the reference room
I watched them
pacing,
heads turning every time the door opened,
pacing
until Spider arrived
to draw them away.

I waited,
fingering hearts,
initials carved into the table,
grinning as I heard myself telling Raymond
of my death-defying escape.

Mail King

Edward MacDermott
came back from WWII
with one good leg,
and got more mail than anybody
in our building,
and read it
instead of watching TV
which he didn't have—
just two empty TV cabinets
crammed with holiday baking recipes
    pet grooming tips
        seed catalogs
            secrets of oral hygiene
plus maps and brochures
from states coast to coast
and countries we'd never heard of.

One wall was half papered with
    a map of China
        a poster of gold leaves in Vermont
            a stain removal chart.
Mail in his lunch pail.
Sundays and holidays his glum days.

Ruth MacDermott,
with Marilyn Monroe lips but rusty hair,
put up with him—
"I suppose he could have been a drunk,"
she told us once—
until Edward received his mail-order snake
and she put her foot down.
"It's the snake or me."

Edward kept the snake.

Ruth wrote postcards
asking if he still had it.
And Edward did
until by mistake he sucked it up
with his Hoover Deluxe.

When we mailed his apology to Ruth,
he said,
"Thanks, fellas,"
handling Raymond a sample of Tide,
me a catalog of garden supplies.

Sisters

Hazel
wore the pants—
bib dungarees,
the trainman's cap—

drove the dirty red Ford
with a green front fender,

never said more than two words at a time
unless it was to complain
about the weather,
the price of groceries,
or the paper
thumping on the porch too late for morning coffee;

raised vegetables—
partial to pumpkins,
cabbage (red and white),
and gourds;

and shooed the cats
if they came within a rake handle.

Emma,
ever the baby sister,
preferred cotton dress
and sweater,
rolled-up sleeves,
straw hat;

rode her bike
when Hazel was in a mood;

rubbed away the paint
on the fence near the gate
from leaning
talking to the mailman,
neighbors,
Raymond and me;

tended the cosmos and tiger lilies
as wind danced
over rows of basil, chives, and tarragon;

planted a patch of catnip
in the sun.

Then came Ed Dutton—widowed,
fast-talking seed salesman
down at the hardware store—
with his proposal
after a band concert
in the church parking lot.
Everybody knew she'd never leave Hazel,
not after all their years, but
she told Ed she needed time
to think.
"I understand," he said
with a nod and a wink
and waited three days
before Emma said she couldn't—
not after Hazel had
washed the truck,
bought a can of shrimp for the cats,
and built a new flower box
for the porch railing.

Bingo

Saturday night
Dad washed, I dried
the supper dishes,
while Mom armed herself
for Early Bird bingo at seven
in the church basement:
her lucky piece
(a smooth quarter she'd won the first time out),
seat cushion,
and a White Owls box of pink plastic markers.

Dad read the paper,
watched TV with me
until Mom returned,
announcing her triumph with a door slam
and a shout,
"I was hot!"

Flinging her hat,
twirling out of her jacket,
she pulled dollar bills
from her pockets
before setting them free
to flutter like fat spring snow.

"Ninety-two dollars!" she squealed
as Dad hugged her off the floor.
"Ninety-two dollars!"

In bed I listened to
mumbled voices
planning to spend the money—
on groceries,
school clothes,
a leaky radiator—
and wished she'd buy
a shiny red dress,
long white gloves,
and clickety-click high heels.

Winner

Mrs. Macey worked behind
the meat counter at Janelli's Market
until her husband took up
with the Methodist organist,
leaving her to wear embarrassment
like split pants.
Then she won the Am Vets' raffle—
a trip to Miami
during the Fourth of July weekend—
and never returned.

Instead
she sent a postcard of flamingos
on the lawn of an awninged hotel
that Mr. Janelli butcher-taped
on the meat case:
"Met a wonderful man
wears a slender moustache,
plays trumpet in a jazz band,
and calls me Cara Mia."

The Kiss

The kiss started when I danced
with Molly Burke,
spelling champ
and crossing guard,
when I could feel
that bumpy bone in the middle of her back
right through her blue dress.

We moved to the punch bowl
where a slice of orange
dropped off the dipper and plopped,
squirting a red flower on a white shirt
my mom had bought the day before.
"Oh my," Molly said.
"It's nothing," I said,
  and sipped
  (tempted to shout,
"They got me!"
  grab my chest,
  and stagger across the room).

We ended up outside
by the pond.
"Moon shadows," she told me
  and pointed,
  but I looked at the side of her face,
  then leaned,
  barely touched
  my lips to the softness.
Her cheek
round as the moon
rose in a smile.